Forgotten Legends

Of the Texas Coast

WILEY MCLAUGHLIN

ISBN: 978-1-732-81969-6

Forgotten Hero's & Legends of the Texas Coast
Lighthouse Series
First Print Edition: October 2021
Volume: 1

DEDICATION

To James Stephenson, my greatest legacy, and his children, the greatest generation and best kept secret of the Coastal Bend.

CONTENTS

ACKNOWLEDGMENTS

Lois Ann Stephenson, for her cheerful and objective views of our family folklore, that James Stephenson was not a disgrace to our family. Jo Ann Morgan held my hand, led me in the direction of fact with fiction folklore, and to seek the real truth. Janet Carpenter, my mentor in all things of manuscript writing. She made me a better author. Liz Mathews, with her knowledge and experience of sufficient detail, I was able to uncover facts and several new historical events lost to the ages. Pat McLaughlin was able to find the land and legal documents that shed light on the truth. Charles C. Butt for giving F.R. Holland, Jr the opportunity to document and preserve the Aransas Pass Light Station, history. Finally, artist Christi Mathews for bringing a local legend to life in her artwork.

Introduction

1
TWILIGHT AND EVENING BELL

It's that particular time of the day if you can call it that. It's past evening bell with twilight just a couple of hours away. Beautiful white sparsely scattered clouds are hanging in that blue sky. There is a welcomed humid breeze coming off the bay. I'm sharing what little shade this mesquite tree gives off with at least seven more old folks like myself. How this old crusted worn-out Pirate and entrepreneur is in the company with these respected town folk and loving family is a long story to itself.

About a hundred of us are gathered here today, this July thirty first, 1891, to say our farewells to a real Texas Patriot and pioneer trailblazer James Stephenson (Death,1891)[1](Obituary,1891)[2]. My god, there must be over sixty family members here today. Several call me "Tio Gaspar," and I love every one of them. They are my family.

I'm standing under this mesquite tree with friends and outlaws. We have all been partners in crime at one time, and every one of us has been called a "Captain." We have Ned and John Mercer, Anderson Jr., Ten Dollar Henry, Max Luther, and Samuel Shoemaker. What a well-rounded bunch with so much in common: domino's, the Aransas Lighthouse, open sea, war, whiskey, and James Stephenson. As we were visiting in the shade, we were all sharing when we first met James. My story was the oldest and the best. I retold the story of how I met Private James and his father, Lieutenant John, on that cold February

---

[1] *Fort Worth Daily Gazette;* Fort Worth, Texas. July 30, 1891, Pg.5, "State Monthly Death's"
[2] *The Taylor County News;* Abilene, Texas, July 31, 1891, Vol.7, No.23, Ed.1, "Obituary"

night in 1835 at the pier in Copano. James handed me that letter from Sam Houston and the bag of Spanish gold coins. You could say that James and his father help me become famous and wealthy on the same day.

Little did I know that it would be almost twenty years later when I met James's wife, Lizzy. My whole life would change for the better. This wayward, lost soul would eventually find love, friends, and family on that day in 1854.

With nightfall coming shortly, these words keep coming to mind.

> "Twilight and evening bell
> And after that, the dark!
> And may there be no sadness
> Of farewell when I embark."3

With that said, we're about to embark on a great party and farewell for old James Stephenson. There will be no tears because tonight Captain, Henry Hawley and his wife Priscilla Stephenson will raise the flag and shoot the cannon in celebration. I am sure a keg of whiskey will be involved.

---

3 Poem: *Crossing the Bar*, by Alford, Lord Tennyson, 1889.

2
FIRST LADIES SARA & LIZZY

Thursday, November fifteenth, 1855, we have clear skies, light winds north northwest calm gulf waters. For a 60-year-old man, quartermaster Smith did an excellent job crossing the bar at Aransas once again. Smith landed the "Sherman" at the Aransas wharf for offload of cargo and re-supply of food and water. It's a quick turn around this trip. We will need to sleep on board and head out at first light for Tampa, Florida, before the next norther.

At the end of the pier, I noticed a new colorful, freshly painted sign. "Sara and Lizzy's Café, 2nd house on the right." It was about that time, so I went to eat. In front of the house to the right of the front door was another sign, "wash hands and wipe feet." A water pail with a hand towel was on a ledge near the front door to the house.

When I step inside, a short and attractive young woman comes out of nowhere and says, "I am Sara, remove your hat and place yourself next to that man sitting in the back corner. Lizzy will bring your plate in a minute". The place was full of customers and laughter, and the food smelled great. I moved to the back and sat next to a tall, middle-aged man with blond hair. He started to introduce himself. "You may not remember me, but I know you, Captain."

About that time, Lizzy showed up with Gaspar's plate of food. Without hesitation, Lizzy said, "When you are finished, take your plate to the kitchen. Don't forget to get a slice of Sara's wild blackberry pie." Then James spoke, "Lizzy let me introduce you to Captain Jose Gaspar. Captain, this is my wife, Lizzy Stephenson." Gaspar stood up. He said, "Madame, it is such a pleasure to meet you, and thank you for

3

your hospitality." Lizzy stuck out her hand and said: "It will be 2 cents and enjoy your meal, Sir". I found in my front breast pocket a 5-cent piece and told Lizzy to keep the change. With a smile and wink, Lizzy raised her voice and said, "Sara, we've got ourselves a polite, handsome, and generous pirate on the premises. Keep an eye out for our children."

As I sat myself back down and began on my chicken stew, James started the conversation; "Well, your respectability and notoriety have increased quite a bit since that cold February morning on the Copano wharf in 1835." Gaspar responded, "Yes, you and your father and of course, a man-call Sam Houston, had something to do with that. Do you remember what I told you on the pier that night?" James continued, "I believe you told me not only did I make you rich, but I also made you famous that night." They both smiled and laughed at the same time.

The conversation went on back and forth for a good thirty minutes; it was like long lost brothers reconnecting again. The crowd thinned out, and it was beginning to get quite in the large room when Lizzy came to the table. "I saved you the last slice of Sara's pie, here take it, now give me your plate, finish-up and get out of here so Sara and I can get ready for tomorrow. Oh, about tomorrow if you would like you can spend the night in our home. You would be bunking with our boys, and you must not keep them up all night filling their heads with wild stories. Supper is at 6:00, lights out at 8:00, and the house is asleep by 9:00. The bed is clean and soft, and you are out of the house before sunrise. Jose, your father he can stay with Sara and Captain William Roberts next door. We will be expecting you at 5:30, don't be late." Lizzy took Gaspar's plate and left. Gaspar turned to James and said, "Is she always like this?" James replied, "I find it best to do as told. Not only is she the mother of my eight children, but she and Sara are also the matriarchs of the Island".

3
LOVE STORY

When Gaspar returns to the "Sherman," he finds Captain William Roberts and two young men talking to his adopted father, Joseph Smith. Captain Roberts turns and says, "Gaspar, I'm glad I found you; let me introduce you to my new pilots and business partners. The tall and stinky one is Frank Stephenson, James's oldest son, and the short one, that's all smiles, is Francis Smith, the outcast and orphaned son of James." The two young men smile and laugh. Roberts goes on, "Frank, Francis, here we have my old friend Captain Jose Gaspar. The third best navigator of these back bays." Gaspar responds, "Well then, that must make you the fourth-best seamen in these parts." With outstretched hands, they smile and give each other a strong hug. Gaspar continues, "William, you must tell me more about these new business opportunities you're working on."

"Well, you know me, Gaspar, too many projects and not enough of me to go around. Captain Clubb and I are still piloting boats across the Aransas Bar. Now I have made two new contracts with Morgan Shipping Company. One from Corpus Christi to Indianola, and another from these docks here at Aransas to the Galveston Central Wharf. Captain Henry Hawley Sr. wants me and Clubb to help with his dreg boat operations around Rockport. Finding work could not be better. That new Lighthouse has really made a much-needed economic impact. I guess you have noticed the six new homes here at St. Joes, and that darn James Stephenson has built every one of them."

Gaspar says, "Next, you are going to want to hire the "Sherman" and crew." Captain Roberts proclaims, "No, just your father, Joseph. I need him to train these two young men and others for me. Gaspar, now don't get upset. I have made Joseph an offer for life." Gaspar asks his father, "Joseph, is this true? Is this what you want?" Then Joseph answers, "Son, I wish to try this. Captain Roberts has made a convincing offer. He has a boarding house behind the Stephenson home, which I am welcome to stay as long as needed, plus I can take all my meals with the Roberts. I get to bunk with my two new students here. Who knows, maybe I will end up in Corpus Christi. Son, this is the right place with good people and a growing and caring community. I don't want to die at sea. You are already coming to this part of Texas at least six times a year; you will be able to look in on me. It's a good fit for both of us." Gaspar answers, "Father, I am glad you chose here. We have made many friends in these parts over the years. Your right. We come back here often. This is a good fit for both of us. I will not hire anyone to replace you. Think of all the money I will save, and as an added bonus, my Captain's room will only have one bed in it. I guess this means I won't be able to order you around ever again?" Joseph smiles and says, "That's right. You are only going to get hugs from me, no more backtalk. I love you, son."

Then Gaspar turned his attention to young Mr. Frances Smith and enquired, "How does one become out-casted and orphaned by James Stephenson? There must be a story here." Frances answers, "Well, yes, sir, there is. If it weren't for Mr. and Mrs. Stephenson, I would not be standing here today. James saved my life about eight months ago. I was the First Mate on the "Arco" while sailing twenty miles out from Galveston Bay. She was destroyed by fire and sank. As far as I know, I am the only survivor. I washed up two miles north from here on St. Joseph Island. James was out on horseback beachcombing when he found me. He told me that I was more dead than alive when he saw me. He brought me home, where his wife Lizzy and oldest daughter Arminda nursed me back to life. It was three weeks before I could open my eyes. I thought for sure I had died (Allen & Taylor, 1997)[4]. When I did open my eyes for the first time, I honestly thought I was looking up at an Angel. She was so fragile and beautiful, all at the same time. When she smiled, it was like the gates of heaven had opened up. It was Arminda Elizabeth Stephenson. I fell in love at that moment.

---

[4] *Aransas The Life of a Texas Coastal County*; William Allen and Sue Hastings Taylor, 1997 Fort Worth, Texas, Eakin Press, pg.97, pages 473.

She and I professed our love for each other four months ago. I ask James and Lizzy for Arminda's hand in marriage when I was outcasted from the Stephenson home. Mrs. Stephenson set the new guidelines for our courtship. I was to leave and live with her best friend Sara Roberts, I would work with Captain Roberts and only see Arminda twice a week. I got the best part of this deal because we have a wedding in seven months, plus I have a great job with Captain Roberts."

4

THIS HOUSE IS BLESSED

Evening came quickly. As I approach the Stephenson home for my 5:30 appointment, I saw three little boys outside playing look like five, eight, and ten years of age. I could overhear the playacting. The oldest of the three was saying, "If you don't do as I command, I will make you walk the plank." From this point forward, I knew I was in trouble. The smallest one saw me first. His eyes got big, and his mouth was wide open with amazement. He was stunned, speechless. The next oldest turned, stared up at me and said, "You are so tall." The oldest one introduced himself and his brothers, "I didn't think you would come. Hello, I am George. These are my two brothers Richard and John Lee." Richard stuck out his hand, So I removed my hat and put it on his head. I picked up John Lee, with his mouth still wide open, placed him under my left arm, and carried him like a loaf of bread. George turned and opened up the front screen door to the house; we marched single file like it was rehearsed. After I got inside, I placed John Lee back to the ground, feet first.

Richard removed the hat and reached up and put it on the hat rack near the front door. There was a bench on the right side of the hat rack. All three boys sat down and started to remove their shoes. As I surveyed the room, it was substantial. A handcrafted dining table was the centerpiece, with eight matching chairs around it. Three windows with handmade curtains, each window had a small table centered in front of them, the tables had fresh wildflowers, and several nick-nacks on each top. There was a large oversized opened entry to the kitchen to my left. A massive fireplace centered the room on the back wall,

9

with three rocking chairs and a doorway to the right corner. James was sitting in a rocking chair and spoke, "You sure know how to make an entrance. Those boys have been waiting for you outside for about two hours. Anyway, welcome to our home. Boys, go wash up and get ready for supper." They all ran into the kitchen. As the boys went in, the girls came out with Lizzy in the lead. I moved closer towards the dining room table.

Lizzy spoke, "Girls let me introduce you to our special guest, Captain Jose Gaspar. Jose, our oldest is Arminda, then we have Mary Isabella, and the smallest is Priscilla." Arminda was just like her fiancée Francis Smith, described her, petite, frail, and a smile that could light up a room. Priscilla was just like John Lee her mouth became wide open. Mary was a brave soul; she walked up to me and said, "Captain Gaspar, it is a pleasure to meet you." Then I responded, "Lizzy, James, thank you for the invite and a chance to meet your family." Lizzy and the oldest Arminda headed back to the kitchen and left the small two girls, just as the boys roared back in the room. The scariest moment in my life, surrounded by five children. I looked over to James and pleaded for help. James smiled and said, "I thought you were a big bad Pirate." James chuckled he continued, "It will do your soul some good."

That's when George started, "I have heard that you are a real Pirate, that you won a pistol duel against one of Jene Lafitte's men, shot him dead, and took his pistol." Gaspar responded, " That is not exactly true, but Captain Cornea did give me his pistol. Look, that's a story for another day. I guess I will not get out of here alive tonight without telling you guys at least one story. I want to tell you a story about a real hero right here in this house, your father." George replied, "We have heard father's stories about how grandpa, uncle John, and dad fought with Sam Houston at the battle of San Jacinto (DRT 1986)[5]."

Gaspar said, "Ok, children listen up and come to the dinner table. I am going to tell you a story that you have never heard before about your father and grandfather. It was nineteen years and six months ago when I first met your father. Did he tell you about that?" All of the children were looking with amazement and wonder in their eyes. Priscilla spoke up, "No, daddy has never said your name before. What

---

[5] *Muster Rolls of the Texas Revolution*, 1986, DRT, Austin, Texas, Daughters of the Republic of Texas, Inc, pages 318.

are you talking about?" George questioned, "Were you at the battle of San Jacinto?" Still standing, Gaspar removed a large leather wallet out of his inside left coat pocket and pulled out an old folded letter. At this point, Gaspar had everyone's full attention. Even Lizzy and daughter Arminda came out of the kitchen and sat themselves down; the children reposition themselves. Little John Lee sat in George's lap. Likewise, the smallest Priscilla sat on Arminda's lap. At the same time, Mary Isabella and Richard shared the same chair's edge between the others. James was still in his rocking chair near the fireplace. Everyone was waiting with anticipation about what was coming next.

Gaspar continues, "I had a cargo for Sam Houston for the war effort. Sam Houston had sent your grandfather and father to the pier at Copano to receive the shipment of guns and ammunition. Your father handed me a bag of Spanish gold coins and this letter." Gaspar unfolded the faded torn letter and read, "This letter is dated February twenty-ninth, 1835. Gaspar, I could not wait any longer. Texas is calling for me. I leave you in capable hands with John and his son James. Texas is in your debt. Thank you, payment is not enough. Signed Sam Houston." Gaspar reached out and handed the letter to Lizzy. With a gasp of disbelief, Lizzy took the note from Gaspar and said, "Oh! my god, the story is true; I had no idea, I thought it was just a tall tale." Gaspar told Lizzy, "I have been holding on to this letter too long. It needs to stay right here with your family." Lizzy passed the letter down the table for the children to see the message for themselves. Gaspar added to his story, "That's not all, there's more. After the battle at San Jacinto. Sam Houston picked sixty-seven men to deliver; the defeated General Santa Anna and Mexican officers back to the Mexican border. Your father was one of those special men (DRT, 1986)[6]. Your father is a real Texas hero."

Gaspar looked over to James in the rocking chair. James smiled and gave Gaspar a convincing nod. At this moment, Jose Gaspar had made lifetime friends with the Stephenson's. He would be considered family from this point forward. Gaspar will watch through time how many of this loving family will become local legends.

After supper and a few more stories, all went to bed. This was the first time since Gaspar had lived at the Basilica of St. Augustine in

---

[6]*Muster Rolls of the Texas Revolution*, 1986, DRT, Austin, Texas, Daughters of the Republic of Texas, Inc, pages 318.

Florida as a young boy had he slept in bunk beds. It brought back good memories. He knew this was where he wanted to be.

The next morning as Jose was sneaking out of the house, Lizzy and James were waiting for him in the kitchen. Lizzy had made a fresh hot pot of coffee. As she was pouring a cup for Jose, she spoke, "Captain, please don't worry about your father. He will be taken care of with love by the community here. I expect to see you often at my dinner table. When you do come to Sara's and my Cafe, you better tip us each time." James added, "Captain, you are welcome in my house anytime, take your cup of coffee and get out of here, and come back soon." Lizzy walked up to Gaspar through her arms around him and gave him a big hug. Then she spoke, "Please, take a bath. My children love you. I want you to be a part of their lives." Captain Jose Gaspar put his hat on his head and told both Lizzy and James, "I will be back in two weeks; thanks." Jose Gaspar never looked back as he left the house. They could not see it, but he a smile on his face the size of Texas.

5
THIS HOUSE IS CURSED

A beautiful warm day, with a light east breeze near the shore at the city of Aransas. It was Monday, March nineteenth, 1860. We came in the family wagon, left our house after lunch, and got here soon after. Mary Isabella and I have listened to Mom and Dad talk as we traveled to the Bishop home. Mother convinced Dad to leave the two pistols in the wagon. Mom said, "Now, James, as we discussed. We leave the guns and butcher knives, in the wagon with George and Mary." Dad replied, "Lizzy, the skinning knife comes with me, and yes, you do the talking."

When we arrived here at Aransas three years ago, from St. Joes Island, Dad had accumulated many parcels of land between here and Liveoak Peninsula. Mr. Bishop, a land agent, was acquiring property for a local railroad developer. The Bishop family were new arrivals to our seaside community. His lousy reputation finally caught up with him about a week ago. He had been doing the same type of work in the State of Alabama, and he was an outlaw. Gossip was that Mr. Bishop and his older son David had several slaves and were currently operating a large Alabama farm. My father only took partial payment for the land, and the transaction had not been completed. Mom and Dad wanted to get the property back. Mr. Bishop claimed that he had improved the acreage, which increased the value, so he would not entertain any changes. That is when the dispute escalated to where we are now.

Mother took the lead to the house. As she got to the front porch, one could hear the crack of rifle fire. Dad instantly recognized what it was and what direction it was going. With a raised voice, "Lizzy, they're shooting at our children. Hurry, we must stop them." Then he screams, "George, Mary, run."

Our mother was first into the house. All she could see was Mrs. Bishop holding a pistol to her side and beginning to raise it. Mom rushed her, knocking her down, and the gun went sliding across the floor. Dad was only a second or two behind her. As Dad made it to the house, a rifle bullet went whizzing from his left to right, narrowly missing his head. Father followed with his eyes to the top of the stairs; it was old Mr. Bishop in the process of reloading the rifle. Dad made the top of the stairs in three giant steps. He grabbed Mr. Bishop at the shoulders with his hands, and both went tumbling down the stairs to the bottom floor.

By this time, Mary and I enter the house, with weapons in hand. I surveyed the room, moved quickly to my mother's side, and handed her my blade. Both Mr. Bishop and Dad have retrieved their hidden knives and start fighting.

On the second floor of the house, younger brother Jacob finds the rifle at the stairs' top step. He takes the gun up and runs to the bedroom where his younger brother David is bedridden, with his final stages of consumption (Ranchero, 1860)[7]. Jacob leaves the rifle for his brother to use if needed and then heads downstairs to help with the family fight.

When Jacob gets to the ground floor, the scene is in chaos. Mother and I are standing side by side, fighting. Jacob moves quickly from across the room and separates all three of us. Mrs. Bishop falls to the floor and passes out. Mom drops her knife and starts crying.

Mary Isabella had been standing near the front door the entire time. With her ax in hand, she climbs up the stairs. Mr. Bishop had several more visible knife wounds and was bleeding profusely. He slumped to the floor and took his next breath with a great sigh. Death was near. As Dad picked himself off the floor, Jacob found his mother's pistol. Father turned to take on the younger Jacob; I knew this might be his last fight. I saw two puffs of white smoke from the barrel of the pistol. Father grabbed his chest with both hands and fell backward onto the floor.

---

[7] *The Rancho*, Corpus Christi, Texas, June 16, 1860, Vol.1, No.35, Ed.1, "Rancho News".

Everything went still and near-silent, then it happened. A single rifle shot from upstairs. Three seconds later, a scream from Mary Isabella, "What have I done." I ran past the front door to the stairs. Out of the corner of my eye, a group of men had assembled outside. That was the longest flight of stairs I had ever climbed. I wish that day had never happened. I could never unsee what was about to unfold before me. That vision would haunt me until my last day on this earth.

When I entered that bedroom, Mary was kneeling at the foot of the bed sobbing while praying, "Father, save me from my sin. Father, save me from my sin." over and over again. Lying next to David Bishop in his bed was the rifle he had used. David's left eye was bludgeoned by the ax. He had a large cut from his upper chest to his pelvis, with the ax blade still in his body. There was very little blood, but his bowels were exposed for all to see (Tragedy, 1860)[8].

I bent over and grabbed Mary by her hands while telling her, "Mary, I am here. We must leave now." Hand in hand, we headed to the doorway of the bedroom. In the hallway, we met two of the men who had entered the house from the neighborhood.

Time had stopped. The next thing I remember was holding my mother three months later. During those three months, both mom and dad spent their days convalescing from their wounds and standing trial for murder (Commissioner's Court Minutes, 1861)[9]. Mother returned from Huntsville State Penitentiary with a pardon given by Governor Sam Houston (Indianola Courier, 1860)[10]. She had a surprise for all of us. A new baby sister would be joining our family in the next few months. It's a long story, but we would not have our father back with us until after the Civil War.

---

[8] *The Standard*, Houston, Texas, April 28, 1860, Vol.15, No.15, Ed.1, "Tragedy".

[9] *Abstracts from Commissioner's Court*, 1961, Refugio County, Texas, January, Micro-film located at Corpus Christi Public Library.

[10] *Galveston Weekly News*, Galveston, Texas, August 21, 1860, Vol.17, No.20, Ed.1, "Indianola Courier Says".

6
SALT HARVEST

It's a bright, and calm September morning. Captain John Anderson and George Stephenson came to the El Mar Rancho yesterday, after a comprehensive survey of the local salt deposits. You know Captain Anderson is always looking for an easy buck from Mother Nature. George reported the time was right for our yearly salt harvest. Frank sent word for me to come by the Ranch and catch the caravan this year. It was such a beautiful morning. An outing with my adopted grandchildren would be fun. I had just finished up breakfast at the Tarpon Inn when John Hope came by in a wagon. John greeted me, "Good morning Tio Gaspar, get in, take the rains, this is your ride for the day, you get the children this trip." With a smile, we were off to the Ranch and then to Salt Lake, near the burned-out Ranch on the outskirts of town. Sure enough, at El Mar Rancho, John Hope had the other wagon ready to go with sacks, shovels, scrapers, water, and sandwiches. Frank Stephenson and Bob de Forest mounted upon horses, our escort for the day. Then it was my turn.

Seven children of all ages descended on my wagon. Let's see, four were from the Stephenson clan, two of George's and both of Frank's. Then there was John Hall, Willie's best friend; he must halve spend the night at George's. To round out the crew were two of Ned Mercer's boys. What a splendid crew it was, maybe the best I have ever commanded. I knew there might be trouble on this short ride (Wood,

1939)[11].

It all started with Willie, George's oldest, "Come on, Gramps Gaspar, tell us some war stories." Then the girls requested, "Please, but this time we want to hear about girl pirates." I told them, "No, not today. I want to tell you children about your parents, uncles, and yes-even aunts, during the Civil War. They are the real heroes. Victory was not theirs. They gained the respect of the community while becoming local legends." The wagon became totally quiet. I had their full attention without bellowing out orders to this crew. I like this. So, it begins.

---

[11] *Corpus Christi Caller*, Dee Woods, 1939, Corpus Christi, Texas, page 11, "Gathering Salt", Historical Reprint from The Dee Woods Collection, Box 6-10, Manuscripts and Notes, Texas A&M University Corpus Christi, Mary & Jell Bell Library,

7

THE LIGHT GOES OUT

You know Willie Mercer; your father came up with a bright idea once. This all starts right over there at the Lighthouse. You could say the Civil War began with the light going dark in 1861. Captain William Roberts was the keeper at that time. He received orders from the Lighthouse District to, remove the lens and secure the Lighthouse station. Captain Roberts was right at forty years old and needed help. So, it was your fathers that came to help. What a gang it was, the Mercers', John, and Ned brought along the two delinquents George and Frank Stephenson. Old Captain Roberts knew disaster was around the corner trying to get this group to work together.

Not a single one of them knew anything about the task evolved. Roberts tried to take command, which was not going to happen. Frank was the smart one; he made sure they brought a single-mast sloop with a rowboat in tow.

First, they were going to disassemble the lens. Second, take each section from the top to the bottom of the Lighthouse using the stairs. Next, carry the lens sections down the long pier to the rowboat. Roberts had no plan after that.

While bringing his part of the lens down the stairs, George thought it would be fun to make it a race. The disaster was already in motion; Captain Roberts could not stop it. Halfway down the stairs, George stumbled, the lens slipped out of his hands and ended at the bottom in two pieces.

After two hours, they had the entire lens on the pier. Roberts asks the boys, "What are we going to do now? We broke the lens (Victoria

19

Advocate, 1940)[12]. Maybe they can order a replacement for the broken piece." Then John Mercer spoke up, "We might as well just leave the broken piece here to be found (Lookout, 1995)[13] (Bangor, 1955)[14]. Then when they find it, they will think the rest of the lens is buried close by." Roberts agreed, "Sounds good to me. Now let's go across the channel to Sand Point and hide it over there somewhere. You boys ponder on that; let's see what we can come up with."

Then a miracle happened, Ned Mercer had an original idea, "Oh, let's take the lens to the Lamar cemetery." Frank Stephenson interrupted Ned, "Even better, how about the old Fagan cemetery and put it next to the hero Captain Bray." See, I told you Frank was the smart one. Captain Roberts agreed, "That's perfect. No one would ever find it. Load it up and set sail to Lamar, and let's pray we don't sink the dinghy."

After the war, the US government rebuilt the Lighthouse. The workmen found the broken pieces in the sand near the base of the Lighthouse. The engineer in charge ordered a new lens, he claimed; even if they found the rest of the lens, it would have been useless. The first light came back in 1867. All of your fathers have kept a code of silence about the matter—end of the story.

[12] *Victoria Advocate*, Victory Texas, January 29, 1940, page 3,:"Lighthouse near Aransas Pass is 84 Years of Age".

[13] *Fort Worth Star Telegram*, C. Poirot, Forth Worth, Texas, September 4, 1995, Sec.B, page 42, "On The Look Out".

[14] *Bangor Daily News*, September 15, 1955, Vol.67, No.77, page 1," Yankees Want It, Rebels to Buy Lighthouse Lens".

8

THE ISLAND IS LOST

Well, let's see. You two girls requested a girly story. Oh, I have a good one. Lydia Leona, this one is about your aunty Priscilla. You kids better keep your mouths shut about this one. If Mrs. Hawley hears I told you her story, she will hog tie me and place me on an ant bed for a month of Sundays. Then John Franklin said, "I believe she would. She can be scary at times." She is an Angel in this story if you can believe that. Mrs. Priscilla Hawley is a true hero.

This all started when John W. Kittredge of the Union began threatening the Fort and citizens of Mustang Island early that summer of 1861. Then, on February eleventh, 1862, he dispatched two small crews to the Island to target Thomas B. Clubb and Robert A. Mercer's homes (Intelilgence, 1862)[15]. The Union Navy destroyed all of their livestock and burnt down their houses. The Island citizens panic, and most began to hide their valuables. These citizens commandeered every boat and evacuated for Rockport and Corpus Christi. The next day the small town looks like a ghost town. Cats, dogs, a few chickens are the only residents left.

On February thirteenth, Kittredge orders his cannons to fire on the earthworks of the primitive fort at nightfall. Captain Neal knows that his thirty-two men are on the losing side of this battle. He tells his men they are on their own; they abandon the fort and try to retreat to

---

[15] *The Times-Picayune*, New Orleans, Louisiana, March 8, 1862, Vol.26, No.36, page 2, "Texas Intelligence".

Corpus Christi. The soldiers become disarrayed and separate into small groups. The three-gunboat Captains set out with their crews and plan an escape. The local Island boys leave to make sure all the citizens have left.

That left eight men in two small boats retreating to the safety of Corpus Christi, uncertain of their fate and not knowing how to get to their destination. None of these soldiers were seaworthy or learned the intricate navigation needed to find Corpus Christi. They would need to sail to the north end of Harbor Island near the coast of Rockport then find the narrow channel of the Corpus Christi Bayou (Weekly Telegraph, 1863)[16].

With no wind that evening, the men had to row. The only possession they had was a single lantern. On the shore behind them was a dark silhouette with lantern approaching the boats. One of the men called out, "Who goes there?" After a long silence, the voice of an angel could be heard by all, "I can show you the way to Corpus." As the silhouette came out of the shadows, the men could see it was a young girl. She was covered in mud. As she enters the boat, she reassures the men, "Even in the dark, I know the way. I have sailed this course, with my brothers both day and night for several years."

This angel of grace navigates the soldiers to the Central Warf of Corpus Christi as promised. Waiting at the dock is Captain Neal and old Captain Clubb. Captain Clubb wraps the young girl in a blanket, and they walk off into the darkness. Captain Neal asks his men what happen. Young Corporal Garza replies, "Sir, we were about one-half mile north of the lighthouse. Then this Mustang Island girl knowing we would need help. Runs by foot through the mudflats of Harbor Island to catch up with us and guided us to this dock." One of the other men added, "By the Grace of God we were saved by this Angel of Mercy. Captain, do you know her name?"

Captain Neal responded, "Let us just call her Grace Darling. Captain Clubb ask me if we would not disclose this young lassie name and leave her out of any reports. We don't want her or their family to receive any ill will from our enemy." So, her legend begins. (Givens, 2017)[17].

---

[16] *The Weekly Telegraph*, Houston, Texas, December 15, 1863, Vol.29, No.39, Ed.1, "Aransas".

[17] *Call Times*, Murphy Givens, Corpus Christi, Texas, May 12, 2017, web on-line edition.

9
WHISKEY AND THE BATTLE

Tere's another story all of you children need to hear. You know, whenever whiskey is shared between the Mercer's and Stephenson's, things just become unpredictable. Sometimes their deeds go a little too far. This story is about just that, the night when whiskey dictated the outcome once again. Maybe you guys can learn from this tall tale.

It started early in 1862 when Kittredge planted his colors over the works on the Shell Bank near Rockport. The Confederacy ordered that all able men and assets return to Corpus Christi and fortify against the nearby Union threat. Major Hobby arrived in town to take over command and work on the untrained and untested small Army.

Hobby starts and finishes with drills all day and every day. One evening, he went out to the tent city to find the soldiers from the Aransas Fort, Company I. He assembled all forty-three men. Then demands, "I need four volunteers for a vital mission." There was dead silence among the man, with no one stepping forward. Then those dreaded words came across his lips, " Corporal Hawley, Second Lieutenants John, and Ed Mercer. Yes, and you First Lieutenant George Stephenson. Step forward, front and center, Company dismissed. (Refugio County)[18]" Hobby waited for the men to return to their tents before he spoke, "You four report to Captain Neal's home for orders, dismissed. Oh, you are not to discuss this matter with

---

[18] *The History of Refugio County Texas*, 1985, Curtis Media Corporation and Texas Extension Homemakers Council of Refugio County, 588 pages, page 68.

anyone, understood?" Then in unison, the four responded, "Sir, yes, Sir."

They stood at attention while Major Hobby walked away. Ned Mercer is the first to speak, "Why are we reporting to our Commanding Camp officer. Why us?" Then Corporal Henry Hawley added, "It's not what we did. George, what are you not telling us? What did you do this time?" George Stephenson responds, "I don't know. Let's go to his home and knock on the door, as ordered." The short six-block walk to their destination didn't come soon enough. When they arrive, Captain Neal's beautiful and refine wife greets them at the front door, and with a raised voice, she announces, "Neal, you have four here to see you. Please don't bring them inside. You four stay on the porch."

Captain Neal comes to the front doorway and addresses the men, "Oh, what do we have here? Yes, yes, yes, I forgot." Then he stepped out to the porch and lowered his voice to almost a whisper as if he did not want his wife to hear. Then he spoke, "I need you four to go to the horse shed; inside you will find behind the stack of hay and underneath the horse blankets — two casts of whiskey. Hide them, and I don't want to know anything. After this is all over, you four return the whiskey as you found it. No one knows anything; we never speak of this. Now go to it." As Neal watched the squad, slipped into darkness, he thought, why did Major Hobby send this squad? He knew firsthand these men loved any whiskey. Captain Neal had a false sense of security about this. No one would ever expect or believe what would happen next.

Ten years later, we find Colonel Lovenskiold, Major Hobby, and Captain Neal playing a dominoes game at the Corpus Christi Fire House. That legendary event came up in conversation between the three. Lovenskiold started by saying, "You know the town folks are still bewildered on how buried unexploded cannonballs, filled with whiskey, are still being found throughout the town (Guthrie, 1988)[19]." Then Major Hobby addressed Captain Neal, "Would that have anything to do with the four misfits I sent, as you requested?" Neal responded, "Well, at least two of the best kegs of whiskey west of the Mississippi, never touch the lips of that devil Yankee, Kittredge. "They

---

[19] *Texas Forgotten Ports*, Keith Guthrie, 1988, Auston, Texas, Eakin Press, page 78, pages 240.

all laughed and smiled. Then Lovenskiold asked, "Neal, did you know what they were going to do?" "No!" answered Captain Neal. Hobby shook his head and added, "My, god, you put a Stephenson in charge. What did you expect?" Neal replied, "They did return one keg. I was lucky to that back." Their laughter was heard throughout the Fire House and on the street below.

Now you know how the mysterious cannonballs of whiskey came to be. Do you know how Captain Henry Hawley helped saved the citizens of this community? That's when Amanda Elisabeth Stephenson asks, "Tio Gaspar, why do some call Captain Hawley, Ten Dollar Henry." Amanda, he received that nickname three years ago. The story goes while playing a card game at the Tarpon Inn. Captain Hawley won a sizable cash pot. He pick-up a ten-dollar bill, put a match to it, and lit his tobacco pipe (Woods)[20]. What a show-off, 'Ten Dollar Henry.' I heard when his wife Priscilla found out what he did that night. She told him he was never to smoke his tobacco pipe in her house, ever again. See, I told you, that woman has a mean streak in her.

---

[20] *Dee Woods*, The Dee Woods Collection, Box 6-10, hand written notes, Texas A&M University Corpus Christi, Mary & Jeff Bell Library.

10
LAST FLAG FOR CORPUS

Let's get on with how Mr. Show Off saved Corpus Christi. On November twenty first, 1863, the order came by horseback from the desk of Major A.M. Hobby to Provost Marshal of Corpus Christi, Colonel Lovenskiold. The Colonel could tell right away these orders were different than any before. It was a small package with a unique seal from Major Hobby's Command. Inside this package were three letters; one for Lieutenant Mann, another addressed to Colonel Lovenskiold, and the last Surrender Decree. Lovenskiold's orders were simple, he asks Henry Hawley to transport Lieutenant Mann on this particular mission.

The next day Hawley was standing on the dock at Rockport waiting for Lieutenant Mann. Hawley's dredge boat was docked at the pier, that morning he sent his crew home and asked if two would go with him on a possibly dangerous mission. Hawley used one of his small sailboats and convinced two crazy volunteers to help with this adventure. Hawley addressed the men, "Let's only bring water, and don't forget the three white flags on the pier there." At the same time, they could see a commotion at the shore. Hawley said out loud, "My god, that's something you don't see every day. Will you look at that, look at that, a gray peacock is coming our way." It was Lieutenant Mann dressed in his most beautiful uniform. No one had seen such an outfit; it was way over the top of any dress regulation. Then one of the crew spoke up, "Henry, you didn't tell us we were going to a party. I am underdressed. Captain Hawley, are you sure about this?" Henry told the crew, "I think this day just got uncertain."

When the Lieutenant got to the small boat, he said, "Captain

Hawley, I hear the enemy has set up command at the Shell Bank. Let us hunt down the Yankees and surrender." Hawley replied, "Yes, sir, a hunting we will go." Even before they left the protected cove, Mann had grabbed one of the flags and was standing at the bow, looking like General George Washington. This was a real sight to behold.

Within one mile, we encountered two small schooners with US colors. The schooners were blockade enforcers. Mann was waving his flag like there was no tomorrow. A call from the nearest vessel, "Halt, what boat is this?" Mann responded, "Flag of Truce ordered by commander Hobby, with a surrender letter." A command came back at once, "Beach your boat and wait for our Captain." The two schooners each had five men and only one officer between them. When the officer came onshore, he walked off into the dry sand with Lieutenant Mann. After a short time, the two returned — the officer left in the second schooner. They left the remaining boat and five crew members. That's when it all went south for Captain Hawley and crew. Three of the Yankee's stayed on shore, holding them at gunpoint. With no officer, they were free to do as they wished. One was loud and started making fun of the Lieutenants dress uniform. They were threatening the crew and calling them names. Then one said, "Hey, throw us a rope, let us find a tree and hang this Rebel Gang." Hawley thought this was his last day on earth. Then something remarkable happened. Lieutenant Mann stepped up and called them out, forcefully with a commanding voice, "You Yankee men will treat us with respect as under the rules of civilized warfare." The Yankee crew brought them aboard while they waited for the return of their officer.

The schooner returned with three officers and five crewmembers. Lieutenant Mann was escorted to the second schooner and taken below deck. Off to the Quarantine Station they went. Henry and the crew were to be transported to the New Orleans prison camp. The Yankees had set fire to Henry's beached sailboat.

That's not the whole story. Then it got crazy. Hawley and crew were handed off to a much larger ship and had set-sail into open Gulf waters when things became strange. One of Hawley's team started laughing while rolling on the ship's deck. He was getting the attention of the crew. Then he could see town folks from Corpus and started strange conversations. He was saying things like, "John Bell would be along soon, we needed to wait for Sam Shoemaker, but it was fine because

Miss Brown had baked a pie." He went on and on. Before they left Texas waters, the Captain of the Union ship ordered the release of this crazy prisoner to shore, for he was not taking any insane man to prison. Anytime Henry Hawley has an audience with a belly full of whiskey, he will re-tell his 'Flag of Truce' story to anyone that will listen (Sutherland, 1916)[21].

This story of the sea reminds me of another great story of bravery and courage—the story of nine brave seamen that had the determination to see the fight to the very end.

---

[21] *The Story of Corpus Christi*, Mary Sutherland, 1946, Houston, Texas, Renin & Son Company, page 23, 146 pages.

11

FIGHT TO THE END

Early in 1865, an order from the Secretary of the Navy from Washington D.C. made its way to the Texas Blockade commanding officer, Captain Emmons. The order was for the destruction of the Confederate schooner "Ann Dale" of Pass Cavallo. The final order of the armed rebel schooner's capture and destruction was given to Lieutenant-Commander Erben of the U.S.S. Pinola.

Commander Erban had sent in several smaller picket boats for the past several months, but the "Anna Dale" could escape and out run anything the Union sent. Finally, Erban sent a gig and third cutter to bring out the schooner and destroy her. Late evening of February eighteenth, the Yankees found their prize moored and all quiet. They were able to slip by two Confederate armed earthen batteries, unnoticed. Lights were seen in the batteries, and men were heard talking. When the cutter got close enough to the "Anna Dale," the Union soldiers jumped on board. Took all crewmembers by surprise and made them go below deck.

The "Anna Dale" was a seventy-five-ton schooner fitted out as a cruiser and full of provisions. In the darkness, the Yankees counted five big launches alongside the "Anna Dale" fitted with torpedoes. The fasts were cut; the vessel drifted into the stream and became grounded. The sail was even made with no better outcome. Decision was made to scuttle the enemy schooner and assessed what they had.

Onboard were nine prisoners with baggage, several small arms, ample ammunition, and one howitzer. Early the next morning on

February nineteenth, the "Anna Dale" was set fire and let burn. Later, when Commander Erban interviewed the prisoners. The master of the crew professed, "I am Joseph Franklin Stephenson, a lieutenant in the Confederate Navy and Captain of the "Anna Dale." He could show no evidence of his rank or authority. Mr. Stephenson continued, "If you were just one hour later. I would have had twenty-five more men. You would have never taken us. At midnight I was to set sail with the launches to Galveston Harbor and do as much damage to your Union fleet as possibly. If I could've found open water, I would've sunk every one of you inside the Pass that night." Commander Erban responded, "Mr. Stephenson, I believe you would have. You were one sly fox and the most difficult adversary I have ever had. But your mine now." The nine prisoners were taken to the New Orleans prison camp (US War Department, 1865)[22]. They were traded in exchange for nine union officers three months later.

Old Jose Gaspar explained to the kids, "You know the Rebels wanted Frank Stephenson and his crew back. His crew was pretty important. These nine men were the best pilot boat captains from the Texas Gulf Coast ever assembled. I would have loved to be part of that crew." Young Charlie Mercer started to cry. The oldest, Thomas William, George's son, asks, "Why the tears, little buddy?" Sniffling while wiping his tears with his shirtsleeve. Little Charlie said, "Guys, we are at the Salt Lake. The stories are over. We got to dig now." Captain Jose Gaspar halted the horse stood up, turned around, and with outstretched arms and said, "You don't worry, little Charlie, we've got the trip back home and children, I've got enough stories of your in-laws and outlaws to last a lifetime."

The End

---

[22] Official Records of the Union and Confederate Navies in the War of the Rebellion, United States War Department, Washington D.C., Series I, Volume 22, West Gulf Blocking Squadron, January 2, 1865 – January 31, 1866, *"Destruction of Confederate Schooner Anna Dale in Pass Cavallo, February 18, 1865"*.

Appendices

Appendix A

Appendix B

Appendix C

Appendix D

Appendix A

Lydia and James Stephenson's Penitentiary Record

James was sentenced to twenty-five years for murder, while Lydia was given five years for second-degree murder. Their term started on May thirty first, 1860, at the Huntsville State Penitentiary in Walker County, Texas. James Stephenson was prisoner #480A, and Lydia Stephenson is prisoner #483A.

Word got out quickly that both James and Lydia were falsely accused, plus Lydia was pregnant. This brought Governor Sam Houston to Huntsville for a personal visit with both James and Lydia. The political environment at this exact moment was chaos for the state of Texas. Succession from the Union was in full motion. Governor Sam Houston was to resign soon, and most of the Texas Legislators and Judges would also leave. Sam Houston told both James and Lydia that a pardon for Lydia would come immediately. Houston explained to James that the evidence of false testimony was so overwhelming that he would be free of all charges soon through the court system. Lydia was pardoned in July of 1860, while James had to wait five and a half years to get his pardon, basically because of the Civil War.

Governor Sam Houston asks Lydia to write him a letter to start the exoneration for her husband, James.

Lydia Stephenson's Pardon

Records of the Secretary of State of Texas, under Gov. Houston: TX State Archives, Austin Ledger 2-1/51

> "*The State of Texas whereas at the Spring term A.D. 1860 of the District Court held in the county of Refugio and the State aforesaid on the 24th day of May 1860, one Mrs. Lydia Stephenson was convicted of murder in the second degree, and sentenced therefore to five years confinement at hard labor in the state penitentiary at Huntsville;*

and whereas it has been represented and made known to me that the said Mrs. Stephenson is pregnant – and I am not willing that any child inherit the disgrace of being born in the penitentiary. Life has ills enough without inflicting them on humanity at its birth – Now therefore, be it known that I, Sam Houston, Governor of the state of Texas, by virtue of the power vested in me by the constitution and laws here of, do hereby grant to the said Mrs. Lydia C. Stephenson a full pardon; and hereby direct the superintendent of the state penitentiary to release and discharge the said Mrs. Stephenson from all further confinement on the account of said conviction and sentence. In testimony whereof, I have hereunto signed my name and caused the great seal of the state to be affixed at the city of Austin, the 21st day of July A.D. 1860 and in the year of the Independence of Texas the twenty fifth.

**The seal of the State of Texas

Lydia Stephenson's Letter to Governor Sam Houston

Texas State Archives, Austin: Box 301-33 folder 66: November the 6, 1860, Liveoak Point

Governor Houston
Dear Sir,
I will pen you a few lines to let you know that I hav reacht home through your kindness whitch pen cannot express the thanks I hav for you. I hav bin in bad health an not able to rite to you any sonner my atorny say there is some ritings to come from you to me he wants me to go to cort as a witness he says I had better have them I would like to hav your advice a litte if you Please be so kind as to do sa Direct to St. Marys Refurio CO

Cort commences next Monday rite soon as you git this an oblige your, Mrs Lydia C. Stephenson

PS I saw you in Huntsvill wher my poor husband yt remains."

There is no evidence or family records that the child she was carrying was ever born. The *"bad health"* mentioned in her letter to Governor Houston must have played a role in that outcome.

Others from the Aransas and Refugio Counties tried to help in the effort to free James Stephenson. Alfred Marmaduke Hobby, a Refugio County elected Texas House of Representative of the Ninth Legislature, wrote the following to Texas State Governor F. R. Lubbock. Before the writing of the following letters, Hobby resigned to enter Confederate military service. Hobby was commander of the Eighth (Hobby's) Texas Infantry Regiment, in charge of coastal defenses between Indianola to Corpus Christi. He became the commanding officer for two of James Stephenson's sons and one son-in-law.

Alfred Marmaduke Hobby's Petition and Letters to Governor F. R. Lubbock

Petition to Governor Lubbock, Texas State Archives, Austin: Box 2-9/458 Rg307, Letter from Refugio Representative, Alfred Marmaduke Hobby:

Goliad July 4th 1862
To his Excellency,
Governor F.R. Lubbock

Sir,

In resigning from my position as a member of the Legislature, there is one duty unperformed, which I owe to a former resident of Refugio County. Last winter, if you remember, I left with you for examination a number of Papers relating to the Stephenson case, which I then explained, in which Hon(?) Pryor Lea and (?) Pickett were interested. These papers contained a unanimously signed petition from the Citizens of Refugio County where the trial of Stephenson occurred. This petition is signed by nearly every reliable man in the county, and many from the district. This headed by the signatures of ten of the twelve juryman who brought in a verdict condemning Stephenson to the Penitentiary, the other two jurymen were not in the county when the petition was being circulated, and there is a certificate from the County

Clerk to that effect. I have been told they would sign it if presented to them now.

As the petition dated some months into the past, I promised (at your insistence?) To circulate another, giving you still stronger fresher evidences of a change in public sentiment, if such existed. On my return from Richmond, I found the County almost depopulated, everybody in the army. There were scarcely? a dozen man there who remembered with any accuracy the circumstances of the trial. They expressed perfect willingness to sign a petition, having for its object the release of Stephenson. Again in conversation with others at the trial, heard the testimony given by Bishop, which convicted Stephenson, I subsequentially reexamined the house in which the fight occurred, do not hesitate to pronounce the testimony false, and so thoroughly is the entire population convinced that Stephenson was sentenced to the Penitentiary by false testimony that they would cheerfully sign any petition to the Executive praying his reprieve (?)

I do not misrepresent the public sentiment of my County in this speaking. I was not at the trial. I do not personally know any of the parties. I am therefore uninfluenced by prepositions and prejudice.

But all seem to agree in thinking that Stephenson has already been pu beyond the magnitude of his offense, if so? I earnest commend him to the clemency of the Executive, I trust that the power so??ly rested in the hands, for the purpose of protecting those, whom, haste, rashness, or false testimony, condemning to unjust punishment, may be exercised in behalf of Stephenson. I would again refer to the petition, it still conveys the sentiment of the Signers – I also enclose a communication on the subject from Judge Hues

I have the honor to be,

Very respectfully your obds. Ser.

A. M. Hobby

Petition to Governor Lubbock, TX State Archives, Austin: Box 2-9/458 RG307: Letter from Rob Hughes: San Antonio June 10th 1862

His Excellency,
F. R. Lubbock,
Governor,

Dear Sir,

Mr. Hobby has informed me that he has or is about to call your attention to a petition in my handwriting presented to governor Clark, just before he went out of office for the pardon of Mr. Stephenson who was convicted of murder of one of the Bishop's in Refugio county.

I was council for the accused and during the trial was convinced that the main witness, Bishop, the father of the man killed, committed perjury in his madness, for the purpose of convicting a man who has only killed in self-defense and I was not the only one who has thought so. He was ???? convicted and sentenced to twenty-five years confinement to the penitentiary.

I refer you to the petition prepared by me – which gives according to my recollection, a true account of the evidence and what occurred afterwards? - ???? the perjury committed. The defense, to show that Stephenson, in killing young Bishop, only fought in self-defense, by the evidence of A.M. Lee brother of Pryor Lee, who is now in the confederate service, ??? circumstances ??? strongly to show that certain ball holes made in the house where the fight took place, were made by a minnie Rifle owned by young Bishop, and were made by the deceased buy a shot from the rifle at Stephenson who was between him and the said ball holes, and it was ???? That near to where the deceased was there was a window which had been closed by nailing an old door shutter over it. This evidence? All bored hard on the evidence of old Bishop, who heard it all. After the evidence of Lee was closed, Bishop was introduced and swore that the shot which made the holes spoken of were made by him by accident. He was standing at the window after the fight was over watching as one of the young Stephensons, who was the beginner of the fight, had gone after the guns of the Stephensons. That from where he stood at the window, he could see through a crack over the window in the direction in which young Stephenson went to return with the guns. While standing at the window with the gun pointed in the direction where the whole was made, he attempted to let down the hammer of the lock, but by reason of loss of blood, could not do it effectively and the gun went off. Mr. Lee was not present when this evidence was given. But viewing? It afterward he informed me that it was false, as there was no such crack above the window as spoken of, and I understand that moral gentleman, true. Judge Devine was one of those. I make the statement from memory, not having seen the petition of papers presented with it when the petition was prepared and there may be inaccuracies in my statement here made. But it is certain, I think, that the truth in its general features is such as I have stated.

I have always thought that Mr. Stephenson was wrongfully convicted and ought to be pardoned. I am satisfied and was satisfied at the trial that he would have not been invalidated in the whole-for such is the rule of law. If he would swear falsely in one aspect, he should not be trusted in an other and then it would stand that Stephenson was either not guilty, or that he was not

proved to be guilty -which is the same thing.
Very respectfully,
Your obl. Se

Rob Hughes

Appendix B

The Grace Darling Story

On the east side of the 900 block, at 912 Mesquite, was the home of Priscilla Hawley, a heroine in the Civil War. When Union forces threatened a Confederate post on Mustang Island, the soldiers there prepared to retreat but the only men who knew the twisting channel around Harbor Island were gone. A 14-year-old girl said she knew the channel and she piloted the boatload of Confederates to safety. Mary Sutherland identified her as "Grace Darling" because she didn't want her name told; she thought her actions "unladylike." She was Priscilla Stephenson who married Henry Hawley.

Murphy Givens
Caller Times
Computer Base Newspaper
May 12, 2017

Appendix C

Order of Prohibition of Alcohol at Corpus Christi in 1862

The Confederate States of America, The State of Texas.

SUB-MILITARY DISTRECT OF THE RIO GRAND.
JURISDICTION OF THE CAMP AT CORPUS CHRISTI, TEXAS

Office of the Provost Marshall
Corpus Christi, June 5th, AD, 1862

To all whom it may concern:

1. The selling of alcoholic, spirituous, vinous, or any kind of intoxicating drinks or Liquors, as well as all trading, bartering or traffic in the same, whether by wholesale or retail, and under any pretense whatsoever, is hereby prohibited.

2. On demand, all persons who have followed such business, are required, to forth with deliver up and surrender to Lieut. Fry, A.A.Sr.Mr. at this Port - all their stock of such articles, on hand, when proper vouchers, showing quantity surrendered and valuation of same, will be furnished to the proper owners.

3. Any violation or revision of this order will be visited on the guilty party with the confiscation and sale of the personal property and effects found open the premises where such violation was committed or such evasion attempted.

Charles Lovenskiold
Provost Marshall

Order for Citizens to leave the Islands

For over 150 years the date and the why citizens of Mustang Island left during the Civil War, have been a mystery. Many historians and authors never could explain this event. I found this handwritten digitized copy at our National Archives. It's plain and simple the citizens, in my opinion, were put under martial law.

The Confederate States of America, The State of Texas.

SUB-MILITARY DISTRECT OF THE RIO GRAND.
JURISDICTION OF THE CAMP AT CORPUS CHRISTI, TEXAS

Office of the Provost Marshall
Corpus Christi, 26th May, AD, 1862

To all whom it may concern:

It is ordered that within the next enduring ten days, the inhabitants of the Islands of St Joseph, Shell Bank, Mustang and Padre, remove from said Islands to the Mainland with their families as well as all their stock and other property.

After the expiration of said ten days, person found upon any said Islands, will be arrested and dealt with summarily; all remaining property will be removed by the Government; and to pay all costs and expenses of such forced removal, a sufficient quantity of such property will be seized to be afterwards, Sold at Public Auction to the highest bidder, for the currency of the country.

Charles Lovenskiold
Provost Marshall

Appendix D

Crew of the "Anna Dale"

Confederate U.S. Civil War Prisoner of War Records 1861-1865
Library of Congress National Archives
ancestery.com/microfilm

Detainment New Orleans, Louisiana
From March 1st till June 1st 1865

Joseph F. Stephenson (Frank) Captain   film #3730

Thomas Foley	film #3697
Frank Hughes	film#3702
John Irca	film #3705
Edward Mercer	film #3714
John Mercer	film #3714
James Mueller	film #3714
Frank Ray	film # 3728
Lconias Riggs	film #3728

All Prisoners above:
Captured February 18, 1865
Confined March 4, 1865
Exchanged April 9,1865

Information compiled by Wiley McLaughlin
June 29, 2017

This is a remarkable group of men. Reveals that Edward and John Mercer were prisoners for a second time during the Civil War. As far as I am aware this is a new fact. The Crew members had no rank, only Frank Stephenson.

ANNOUNCEMENTS

From the Lighthouse Series

The Lost Keeper: A Short Thriller by Wiley McLaughlin, second printing 2018

A Pirate for Texas: The Story of Jose Gaspar by Wiley McLaughlin, 2018

The Island Mustang: Danish Folk Tale by Wiley McLaughlin 2017

The Island Mustang

The Island Mustang is a sinister animal and is said to lurk close to shore. This beast is found in a maze of dunes. Accounts tell that it can appear as a gleaming white stallion. Some reports claim it can change to a bright silver or gray. When people get close enough, they will realize this is no ordinary horse; his mouth is full of razor-edged teeth, which can rip you to shreds. Its beauty often fools children, and they all want to ride him. It doesn't matter how many wish to climb on his back, for the horse's back can grow to any length to accommodate every child that wants to ride. When all the children are seated and comfortable, the Island Mustang will gallop into the water, never to return to shore.

By Wiley McLaughlin

©2017

Keeper of Lydia's Light

Christi Mathews – Artist
digital copyright held by Wiley McLaughlin © 2019

The above painting is the Aransas Pass Light Station at Port Aransas, Texas. Frank Stephenson is standing on the pier in 1893. Stephenson was Assistant Keeper from 1892 to 1897 and Keeper until 1917, he holds the longest tenure at twenty-five years.

www.ingramcontent.com/pod-product-compliance
Lightning Source LLC
Chambersburg PA
CBHW030510100426
42813CB00002B/420